# BUILDING MISSIONARIES

## fostering souls for success on the field

### GLENN HANNA

**urban**press

**Building Missionaries**
by Glenn Hanna
Copyright © 2018 Glenn Hanna

ISBN # 978-1-63360-096-6

For Worldwide Distribution      Printed in the U.S.A.

Urban Press
P.O. Box 8881
Pittsburgh, PA 15221-0881 USA
412.646.2780
www.urbanpress.us

This book is dedicated to my wife Patricia, my greatest blessing since Christ.


Thanks to Dr John Stanko for your encouragement and expertise throughout this project.

Thanks to Miriam Oren for your diligent editing and loving sacrifice.

A special greeting to the many workers who own my heart. This book is a result of the deep love that the Lord has given me for each of you. As I frequently say, I am privileged to walk with giants.
Where you go, you all take my heart with you.

# INTRODUCTION

This book is written for any pastor, missions committee chairperson, missions mobilizer, youth pastor, or parent who has been bewildered when some beautiful, bright-eyed, pure-of-heart, idealistic, full-of-hope young person has approached them and said in a quiet voice, "I think maybe God is calling me into missions." Your next thought is "Wow, great! How in the world do I handle this? What should I do?"

Most of us are comfortable pointing them to a denomination's missions department (if they have one) or to a sending agency that is active in the part of the world to which the person feels called. I assure you that this is an inadequate response. There is nobody on the planet who has the time, relationship, or capacity to do what you will be able to do. This potential missions candidate is a member of your church family, and you may know their family and friends. You may know things about them that will never be discovered in a group preparation meeting at the sending agency.

Even more important is the fact that you may have already invested in this person's life and development with love and care in ways that no one else could have done, and this person has a trusting relationship with you. If you have not, their call to missions may open the door for you to do so. Either way, you will build a deep bond with the candidate that will last a lifetime. You will become the confidante and advocate who may make it possible for them stay on the field and win an entire nation or people group to Christ.

I am a 66-year-old missions pastor. I started my career in the steel industry around Pittsburgh in 1975 and worked in business and industry for most of my adult life until 2004 when the youngest of my five children left for college. I hit my mid-life crisis with a thump at the age of 51, wondering what could possibly be next in my life that would give me as much joy and fulfillment as raising my five wonderful kids. I had plenty of business setbacks and losses that convinced me my fulfillment was not to be found in the business world.

While praying and seeking God in that season of life, I heard a clear and certain call to ministry. I knew I did not want to be the pastor of a church, because I do not have the patience or personality for that. I thought I could possibly use my business background to teach job skills to inner-city kids in a business context. I began planning a manufacturing business to fit that purpose and went back to school to get a ministry degree in

Christian community development.

Before I got to the point of building the business, the executive pastor of our large, inner-city, and diverse church asked me to step in and take a position as the community development director. Eventually I was appointed as the missions pastor, and so I entered this new position in 2008 with no missions experience.

When I was appointed the missions pastor, I asked what the position required and was told that I would need to write my own job description. I went on the Internet to research just what a missions pastor does. In the intervening years, I have learned how to do the job and, thanks be to God, He has given me great grace that enabled me to build a valuable and successful program and department. At the time of this writing, we have more than 40 people from our church serving in missions around the globe and another 40, aged 13 to 60, who are at some point in the preparation process.

## My Greatest Challenge

This book addresses the issue that has become my greatest challenge and defines my most important duty as a missions pastor, and that is to mentor and prepare these called ones for a life on the field.

Our church donates over one-sixth of its annual budget, representing well over a million dollars, to missions. This figure includes only those donations we know of. I suspect there is much more we will never know about. While I am involved in raising missions awareness and even occasionally raising money for missions, nothing I do is anywhere near as important or as globally and eternally impactful as mentoring and preparing missions candidates.

This book is not a formula for producing

successful candidates. It is a guide and philosophy for a discipling relationship that opens the door to intimacy and transformation in the candidate enabling them to minister effectively in the most extreme places on earth.

## THE GOAL IS NOT A PERFECT CANDIDATE

There is no such thing as a perfect missions candidate. The goal is a healthy, growing, and self-aware candidate who is equipped for the battles that lie ahead. This book should not be used in a sequential way. Not every candidate will necessarily need to work on every aspect or every detail found in this book. Instead, this book should be used as a guide to assist the mentor in determining what weaknesses or strengths each individual candidate may have.

For example, you may have a candidate who comes from a solid Christian family background and is also theologically sound and emotionally stable, but is lacking in ministry engagement or lacks confidence or social skills. You may find a candidate who is passionate about missions but is theologically ignorant.

I encourage you to use this book as a guide to dig into the candidate's life so you can use your own gifts and resources to equip them for success on the field.

Glenn Hanna
Pittsburgh, PA
October 2018

# chapter one
# THE RATIONALE

I became a missions pastor because I was passionate about missions and our church had decided we needed someone in that role. Over the previous 35 years, our 100-year-old Christian and Missionary Alliance church has been led by Pastor Rockwell Dillaman. Rock is a passionate visionary who had come to our all-white, inner-city Pittsburgh C&MA church with a vision to transform it into a church that reflected the racial, economic, and ethnic diversity of our neighborhood.

He and the staff of Allegheny Center Alliance Church (ACAC) worked hard for many years to develop a church that was passionate about community development, racial reconciliation, at-risk youth, and community-oriented children's ministry, just to identify a few of its values. In the process, ACAC helped to start businesses, a medical clinic, purchased and closed a nuisance bar, served the local population in many ways, and engaged with the community in economic development. ACAC also now reflects the racial, generational, and economic diversity of the Western Pennsylvania community.

During those years, our church continued to be deeply engaged in global missions, but the passion for outreach drifted toward the local community, somewhat at the expense of our global responsibilities. This resulted in the request for me to become the first-ever missions pastor at ACAC.

In my first year as the missions pastor, as I felt my way through the enormous task before me, I began to mentor my first missions candidates. I had a sense that I needed to prepare these young people, but really did not know what I was doing. The first young person had come to me with a desire to go to the mission field with an established agency. She had a master's degree in her chosen field. She was bright, articulate, well-educated, and passionate. She was fluent in the local language of the field and had been to her country of interest and continent several times previously for extended stays. Let's call her Kim.

I met with Kim at our regularly-scheduled weekly meetings to work out the details of her intermediate-term call to the field. I helped her settle the plans for the trip and work out the details with her chosen agency. I also met with her to discuss her life and calling. In the meetings, I noticed a few things that gave me some cause for concern, but because she was such a well-educated and clearly competent person, I overlooked them.

Kim did deploy to the field, and almost immediately things began to go wrong for her. When she arrived on site, there was nobody to greet her. The field director, who had promised to meet her at the airport, instead was in the United States resigning her position. She had failed to inform the team on the field that Kim was coming for an extended stay. The medical doctor with whom Kim was to work while on the field was in prison on trumped-up charges of distributing expired medications. Kim had not been informed of this rather important detail.

There had been no living arrangements made for Kim. She ended up staying in an apartment owned by the agency that was severely flea-infested, so Kim had over 250 fleabites at any given time. She was assigned to work with a team that was dysfunctional due to infighting and jealousy. Kim became the object of the team's dysfunction and the focus of their ridicule.

These issues and many others, combined with Kim's tendency toward depression, low self-esteem, and paranoia served to concoct a dangerous cocktail of harmful thoughts and actions. Kim, like all missionaries and ministry leaders, became the target of the enemy. Satan and his demons attacked Kim in many ways. She found herself isolated, unprepared, and ill-equipped to fight the enemy.

I was stunned by these occurrences but quickly realized this dangerous position she was in was entirely my fault. The Lord had clearly shown me some red flags, but I ran right past them. I had seen indications of her frailty and lack of stability in our discussions prior to her deployment. I had not questioned or pursued these issues, however, because of her poise and apparent professionalism and educational preparation. I had sent a warrior into the enemy's camp and into intense spiritual combat without preparing her for the warfare that she, and all missionaries, inevitably encounter.

The good news is that she survived. She came home after 10 months on the field. She was depressed, humiliated, infected with parasites, harassed by demons, disappointed, haunted by accusations of failure by the enemy, and worst of all, defeated by a belief that she had missed God's call and that He had let her down.

Again, this was my fault. I had let her down. I had failed to dig deeply into her past and present to find the vulnerabilities that the enemy would exploit for the purpose of destroying this beautiful and eagerly willing servant of our Lord.

God has forgiven me for this but taught me a valuable lesson in the process. I may send someone to the field in the future who is ill-prepared, but it will be despite my best efforts, not because of negligence.

## THE FAILURE OF PRE-FIELD TRAINING

It is largely accepted in missiological circles that one of the greatest failures of most missions-sending organizations (MSOs) and missions-training institutes is the failure to adequately prepare candidates for the field. This is not a new problem and if you are interested in the topic, there is a wealth of published material to support this statement.

A friend of mine was a lifetime missionary and country director for a wonderful sending agency. He and his family had spent many years on the field. He confided in me that this failure of pre-field preparation was in his opinion a huge matter. In a conversation on the subject, he stated that during his last years on the field, three out of three married couples that the agency had sent to him were so ill-prepared each of them had lasted less than a year on the field. They had all failed due to lack of appropriate preparation. The issues that sabotaged them could easily have been resolved or discovered prior to their deployment.

Many MSOs do a great job of pre-field cultural training. They also are good at screening candidates for specific job skills as well as for calling and passion for a specific field or work. Colleges and seminaries similarly are great at preparing candidates theologically, culturally, and educationally for the field. None of these institutions, however, are necessarily well-equipped to prepare a candidate psychologically, spiritually, or emotionally for the challenges of full-time, cross-cultural ministry. Neither are they able to discover the subtle or hidden things that the enemy will certainly exploit when that candidate eventually gets to the field.

Most people are raised in less than perfect family and community situations. We all suffer scars and wounds from family, friends, or outside influences as the result of bigotry, poverty, privilege, various types of abuse, divorce, learning disabilities, deaths in the family, abandonment, illness, or a million other trials, sins, or dysfunctions. Theological education cannot address or fix these issues. As we grow and cope in an imperfect world, we devise means for survival that frequently suffice to get us through various trials as a child or adolescent, but that cannot serve us well as adults.

In the severe and intense world of cross-cultural missions wherein a person leaves home, family, familiarity, and culture for loneliness, strangeness, isolation, and hostility, any weaknesses and insufficient coping mechanisms will explode and fail. The results can be failure on the field at best, or long-term breakdown or even death at worst.

## Great News

The great news, if you are a pastor or missions leader, is that the Lord has provided you. He has equipped and enabled you to do this great task that nobody else is doing and probably are not capable of doing. You are in a unique position to pour life, love, and knowledge into these candidates in a way that no one else can.

It may be that the candidate will come to you at age 12 and you will have the next 10 years to build them into a missionary warrior, or they may come when they are 26 and planning to leave for the field within the year. Either way, you are in a unique position to pull them close to yourself, to stick your nose in their business, and to examine all the parts of their lives for the purpose of exposing weaknesses and building up their capacities for the warfare that lies ahead.

The closer a person is to deploying to the field, the more intense should be your engagement with them. In my work, I make and take it very personally. I have candidates I meet with weekly, others biweekly, and still others on a monthly basis. I train other people to mentor as I am doing so we neglect nobody. For me, this is a life-and-death duty that I take quite seriously.

As I get to know a candidate, I consider that every area of their lives is my business. I do not allow them to keep secrets from me. I do not allow them to tell me that something hurts too much to examine. I do not allow them the luxury of shame or remorse. Everything is my business.

I hold them accountable and force them to examine every part of their lives. This can only happen in the context of a committed, loving, safe, and trusting relationship. For some, this may be the first such relationship of their lives. There will be more about this later. The great news is that you can build successful and happy missionaries with whom you will have a deep and abiding loving friendship for the rest of your lives.

## Caution - Attention

Not every candidate is going to be interested in going through your boot camp. There are some who will turn you down flatly. I had a woman from our church who deployed to the field last year, and I didn't even know her nor that she was considering going to the field. I had a young woman several years ago who walked into my office and told me that she was moving to Guatemala the following week and asked if I would pray for her. I said I would but suggested we first sit down and have a talk. She had come home from a short-term trip to Guatemala several weeks earlier with a conviction that God was calling her to move there. She promptly sold all her belongings and arranged to move.

Several years ago, there was a young man with whom I was working, I suggested that I mentor him as he prepared to go overseas to a difficult field. His response was that he thought mentoring would be a good idea, but he wanted to be mentored by someone whom he respected. His clear implication was that I was not someone who fit that category.

Rather than taking offense or insisting that I mentor him, I talked with another more experienced pastor and asked if he would be willing to mentor this candidate. He agreed and had an opportunity to pour two years of valuable care into this young man's life. I have remained good friends with the candidate and we stay in regular contact. I love him dearly and pray for him regularly.

Be aware that people who respond to a radical call to missions are frequently independent-minded people. They are confident and courageous trailblazers. Their tendency will be to get to the field as soon as possible and be done with the dallying. My advice is to take what you can get. Do what you can. There will be issues you see that seem important to you, but your candidate will dismiss and refuse to address. Take what time they will give you, trust that the Lord loves them more than you do, and do your best.

This intense discipleship and mentoring are not only things you *should* do but also things you *can* do. The remainder of this book will set the mood for you so you can see how easy and commonsensical this process is. I like to tell people to engage this process as they would hope someone would do to prepare their own beloved child for the field—and it all begins by getting to know the candidate(s).

Knowing everything about the candidate will be your first and ongoing priority. When someone comes to me and expresses that they think God is calling them to the mission field, I pull them close to me so I can get to know them. The first thing I do is set up a meeting for at least an hour to make friends with the candidate. I ask a lot of questions. I want to know why they think they have a call to missions. If after this first meeting I agree that God has a call on the candidate's life, I set up regular meetings with them every week or every other week.

Over time, you will want to explore every area of the candidate's life. Therefore, you will need to get comfortable with asking probing and sometimes intrusive questions. Explain to the candidate the danger of the call to missions and that the enemy will seek to exploit every weakness in them. Convince them that the enemy seeks only to steal, kill, and destroy. Satan does not seek only to distract or render them useless; he wants them dead. This is the rationale for your intrusive and invasive questions.

Following are some areas of enquiry that must be opened. This is not an exhaustive list nor is it intended to be. As you get to know the candidate well, there will be many issues, attitudes, and perspectives that arise and need to be examined. Here are some things you will want to know.

## FAMILY HISTORY, INCLUDING RELATIONSHIP WITH SIBLINGS, PARENTS, GRANDPARENTS, ETC.

This is of the utmost importance. You may discover that the candidate does not get along with any of his/her siblings and is convinced that both parents have never understood him or her. This may be true but do not accept it at face value. This may be an indicator that there are authority issues, rebellion, pride, aloofness, or an unwillingness to admit sin or guilt. Any of these will show up on the field and disrupt a team or cause the candidate to fail in other ways.

## RELIGIOUS HISTORY OF ALL FAMILY MEMBERS

Examine this area quite thoroughly. False religions are frequently attended by demons who may have a foothold and will beguile or corrupt the candidate. These may include Jehovah's Witness, Mormonism, or any other false or animistic religion. There may be New Age philosophies or other cult influences that have played a role in the candidate's past or present.

## AUTHORITY IN THE HOME, MOTHER TO FATHER, CHILDREN TO PARENTS

If the candidate does not understand or recognize authority, this will be disruptive to the team on the field and may render them useless to the Lord—and a problem for those already serving there.

## FORMATIVE EVENTS LIKE ILLNESSES, DEATHS, DIVORCE, TRAUMAS, FAMILY, DEFINING EVENTS, DISABILITIES, ECONOMIC SETBACKS, ETC.

These formative events can be helpful as maturing tools the Lord will use to build wisdom, stamina, and maturity into the candidate. They may also be tools the enemy will use to undermine the candidate. I know a woman who lost her father at the age of six. This was an obvious life-altering event that caused a great deal of chaos in her family. There was lots of arguing and fighting among her siblings and her heartbroken and traumatized mother.

The young girl could not face the intensity of her losses and the danger of her family life and so she withdrew. She spent all her time at home in the safety and peace of her bedroom where she occupied herself with her personal fantasies. She developed a strategy for coping with life that included withdrawal from all conflict. This served her well as a seven-year-old but undermined her life as an adult.

Seek out these issues in your candidate. Dig deeply and if you find something that causes you concern, expose it and find a way to get the candidate the help he or she needs.

## WORK HISTORY OF PARENTS

Was the candidate able to rely on the provision and protection of predictable parents? This issue has shaped a person's understanding of God and His faithfulness.

## WORK HISTORY OF THE CANDIDATE

Does the candidate show initiative and take responsibility? It is cause for concern if a person has reached the age of 22 and has never held a job or been responsible for their own maintenance.

## FAMILY VALUES, ETHICS, AND VIRTUES

Sometimes family ethics or values can place undue pressure on a person. The danger is that these family virtues, though possibly good, may become confused with godly virtues and the candidate can become upset and disoriented when they are not present.

I worked with a young woman who was internally compelled to overwork and overachieve. When I questioned her about this over time, she stated flatly that her family always worked the hardest and longest. This was an ethic passed down by her parents that had the potential to undermine her success here or on the field.

## DRUG OR ALCOHOL ABUSE, EATING DISORDERS, OR OTHER ADDICTIVE TENDENCIES

Explore these directly and with frankness. Find out what the origin of the temptation was or is. What was the state of mind or life that allowed substance abuse to be a possibility? Was there a triggering event? What is the likelihood that this may re-emerge? If a similar trigger should happen on the field, is the candidate solid enough to survive?

I was working with an excellent young woman who had developed an eating disorder on two previous occasions while in college. Both were related to failed relationships with boyfriends. We paused her preparation to go to the field until we were certain that this would never again be a possibility. We directed her to Christian counseling and supported her through the healing process. She is now once again moving toward fulfilling her calling to the field.

## SEXUAL MISCONDUCT OF PARENTS OR SIBLINGS

This can have a deep and powerful impact on children. If a father has been a pornography addict, or the mother or father has been an unfaithful spouse, the children do not have the means to understand this or the resultant disruptions that occur in the home. It can cause a daughter to question her value, acceptability, or attractiveness. It may have given license to sons to misbehave sexually. It can destroy a daughter's self-image or her understanding of why she is valued by God. There may also be an acceptance of ungodly beliefs such as "all men are unfaithful," "you cannot trust anyone," or "this happens in all families."

## EDUCATIONAL VALUES OF FAMILY; PRESENCE OF ANY BIGOTRY OR CHAUVINISM

Is the candidate a learner? Does he or she have a curiosity and flexibility that will allow him or her to grow in love and appreciation of a different culture? Is there a desire to know the unusual and to delight in cultural diversity? Is the candidate able to separate Christianity from American culture and colloquial prejudices and preferences? Many failures on the mission field have resulted from an arrogance that stems from cultural preferences and bias. Help the candidates identify their own biases.

## PERSONAL LIFE

Discover everything you can about the candidate's life: his or her habits, interests, passions, preferences, reading habits, movies, television, friends, hobbies, sports, music, and art, etc.

## WORK HISTORY

How do they get along with their boss? If they are always struggling with authority, this must be addressed. People who have not learned to submit to God's appointed authorities in their lives will cause problems for the work on the field.

How do they get along with coworkers? If this is a problem, it will also be a problem overseas. If you discover a critical spirit or a contentious attitude, address it and help the candidate get freedom. If not dealt with, this will produce isolation and contention on the field.

How do they get along with their subordinates? If you discover that the candidate cannot seem to get cooperation from their subordinates or there is always frustration in these relationships, find out why.

Can they keep a job? Why or why not?

## FINANCIAL HISTORY

Debt? Many missions sending organizations will not allow candidates to go to the field if they are carrying debt. Is the debt college-related? If not, what is the reason for the debt? Does the candidate know how to manage their finances? Accountability? Does he or she pay their bills? Do they live within their means? Why or why not?

## Sexual history

Are they living a chaste life if single? You must know their thoughts about sexuality. Are these thoughts consistent with biblical teaching? Have they had a promiscuous life in the past? Why or why not? Both questions are important to know.

Was there any promiscuity prior to salvation or post salvation? If the candidate was promiscuous prior to salvation, discover the thinking that led to the decision to be promiscuous. If it was after salvation, dig deeply. What allowed him/her to disregard the Holy Spirit and what needs were unmet? Explore this completely. Discover what allowed them to betray their principles and God's commands. Require counseling with a trusted Christian counselor if satisfactory answers are not forthcoming or if these issues do not appear to be resolved.

If married, are both spouses faithful in the marriage? If not, you must demand obedience. If it is in the past, discover the circumstances and the resolution. Then require counseling with a trusted Christian counselor if necessary.

## Pornography

Most young men struggle with it. It is necessary that this be conquered and renounced along with the demonic, habitual hold associated with pornography. Ask the embarrassing questions. Do not assume that the issue, once addressed, is resolved. This will explode and destroy many on the mission field.

## Education

Get to know your candidates and their educational choices and interests.

## LEARN THEIR SELF-IMAGE
## AND MOTIVATIONS

This can be determined by their statements that begin with "I am a" and then they fill in the rest of the sentence. For instance, "I am an athlete," or "I love opera," or "I am a musician and I love to perform." The question is how will this affect the candidate's capacity to find fulfillment on the field. If the candidate is an avid reader and consumes several books per week, how will he or she adjust to a lack of reading material?

I had an eager young candidate who signed up for an intermediate missions stay in a Middle Eastern country. This young woman was an outdoors person to the extreme. She loved mountain and rock climbing. She spent her free time traveling the world seeking the most challenging and extreme climbs on earth.

When she returned from her time in the Middle East, she came to my office and wept many tears saying, "I just cannot live my life in a burka. I am willing to carry Bibles over the Himalayas or live in a grass hut, but I cannot wear a burka for the rest of my life."

This is the reason you want to discover the candidate's passions and how this might relate to their understanding of their call. Consider areas like the following:

- Sports
- Habits
- Music and art
- Personality strengths and weaknesses
- Fears
- Goals
- Bucket-list dreams

## EXAMINE THEIR
## RELATIONSHIP WITH GOD

This includes their philosophy and practices of:

- Worship patterns and preferences
- Prayer and Bible study habits
- Sabbath and rejuvenation
- Refreshment and restoration

Even though I presented this material in step-by-step format, I am not suggesting that you approach the candidate with the clipboard checklist, like a pilot would approach his or her pre-flight list. However, I do mean to say, however, that nothing is off limits. It is all important so you have as good a profile of your candidate as possible.

As you begin to compile this overview of the candidate, you will have completed the initial steps, but there are many more steps to come. You will use this profile to develop your strategy to mentor the potential missionary. Let's continue with the next steps in Chapter Three.

## chapter three
## YOUR ROLE

This first phase of mentoring is critically important and never really ends, but will continue throughout your relationship. As you go on, many issues will arise that will warrant additional exploration. For instance, changes in job status, friendships, or family relationships may occur, all of which will need to be discussed and processed. You will need to be aware of all the details of the candidate's life. Though all these may not need your pastoral input, you still must be aware of the impact of the events as well as the capacity of your mentee to resolve these in a godly and healthy way.

### BE A REAL PERSON

Keep in mind that your goal is to enable the candidate to become a victorious Christian servant. Therefore, it will be necessary for you to be open, honest, and transparent with the candidate. Freely share your trials and struggles. Recognize that they will be as honest and open as you are. If you have struggled with sexual issues like lust or other temptations such as anger or fear, talk freely and openly but also appropriately about your struggles and victories. Stress the freedom that you have found and give God the glory for setting you free.

This will help them realize that they are not an ugly, sinful anomaly in God's kingdom but a normal Christian sinner set free by the grace of God. Your openness will also allow them to relate to you on a human level and will help them see that God uses broken sinners saved by grace to accomplish His will.

Remember that the candidate will respect you as an authority and will appreciate you as one who is able to move him or her closer to achieving their dream of serving God overseas. If you, their pastor or missions leader, can serve God well even though a flawed sinner, it will give them hope.

## THE BIBLE IS THE FINAL AUTHORITY

The source and foundation for your counsel and teaching must always be the Bible. As each event or crisis warrants, the mentee must always be directed to Scripture to find resolution or to a counselor who works from a sound biblical worldview. Each life event is an opportunity for you to direct the candidate back to God and enhance their relationship with and trust in Him.

It will never be sufficient that our opinion, cultural bias, or generational perspective be the reason we direct someone else to change. Frequently, our mentees will have grown up in a different cultural context than we have. Their understanding of the world may be very different than ours. It may or may not be better. Nevertheless, we should never expect them to conform to our predispositions simply because they are our personal preference. The basis and reason for change and improvement must be grounded in Scripture and reasonably presented and defended.

It is also necessary to allow the Holy Spirit to work through you. Do not expect just because something is plain and clear to you or because you consider your explanations to be perfect and above reproach, that you should be able to argue somebody into an acceptance of the truth. Present the truth to the best of your ability and then allow God to convict and convince. He is far better at convicting the world of sin than we can ever be.

## Don't Assume Anything

*Do not assume because you have addressed an issue that it is therefore a settled issue.* As you discover weaknesses or besetting sins in your candidate, address and then regularly revisit those issues. If you find fear, revisit the topic of fear frequently. If you discover masturbation and pornography, frequently ask about their victory over these sins. It is your persistent love, support, and call to accountability that will enable them to move more quickly to victory and maturity.

After more than 40 years of walking with Christ, I still struggle with some of the same sins that plagued me 40 years ago. My sin tendencies have remained remarkably consistent. I have never struggled with theft and so I am never tempted to steal. But when I drift away from a deep and close relationship with Christ, and am inconsistent in my prayers and devotions, the old temptations raise their ugly heads again and again. Satan knows my vulnerabilities and weaknesses so that is where he tempts me.

The purpose of all the preceding information is to help you imagine your role as a mentor, leader, accountability partner, and discipler. These explorations will help you see what needs to be done to properly prepare the candidate. There is no such thing as a one-size-fits-all approach.

As you proceed through these matters, you must be very prayerful. Information about the candidate will never be sufficient for you to do your job well. You must also be an intense intercessor on behalf of the candidate. You will need discernment, wisdom, and insight to be able to see past what is presented by the candidate to what the Lord sees. This happens in the context of a deep, ongoing, and focused intercessory commitment on your part and on behalf of the candidate.

You may be the only person lifting the candidate up before the Lord. You may be the only person who knows what the individual is facing. With all this personal information comes the duty to lay the candidate on the altar before the Lord and cry out on his or her behalf.

I frequently find myself praying for one of these candidates when my words fail and I can do nothing more or better than to silently hold them in the presence of the Lord with tears running from my eyes. I am left without words and have nothing more than an intense groaning deep in my spirit. In these moments, I trust the Lord knows what is needed far better than my inadequate words can express.

After all, it is the Lord who will bring maturity and

the Holy Spirit who will bring about eternal change. We are at best the instrument God will use to accomplish His will. This leads us to the next and even more important matter you must address with your candidate, and that is intimacy with the Father.

## chapter four
# A RELATIONSHIP WITH THE FATHER

Though Bible colleges and seminaries educate and instruct in matters related to theology and other ministry-related topics, there is no guarantee that a graduate will have developed the disciplines or the passions necessary for an intimate relationship with the Father. In fact, it is quite possible that the opposite may occur. There are many stories of people who enter a seminary with a passionate love for God and exit with a cold and academic understanding of the Father. Their deep, passionate love is replaced by a systematic thought process and analysis of the attributes of God and His interactions with mankind.

Because leaders are often intelligent and highly educated people, we drift towards a reliance on our own strengths in ministry rather than a dependence on the

Holy Spirit and His empowerment. We analyze new situations in the context of our experience and training, and search our cerebral database to select appropriate actions out of our own proven capacities.

For example, I am a builder. I spent many years in the construction industry as a carpenter, construction manager, and contractor. Because I have broad and extensive experience, I do not need to pray much about how to build something. I know good building practices, building codes, and state-of-the-art techniques. I have learned through study, trial and error, the experience of experts, and my own failures. I never need to stop and pray about where I should drive a nail. I just know.

Expertise is a wonderful gift, and we should be grateful to God that He enables us to learn, grow, and become experts in a chosen field. This same ability to gain expertise, however, can become a hindrance to ministry. If we as ministers or missionaries begin to think our education or expertise can make us sufficient in ourselves, then we are in danger of attempting to do God's work in the flesh rather than by the power of the Spirit.

I have a great opportunity as a missions pastor to travel the world and work with many missionaries. Frequently when I am overseas, I have opportunities to sit and connect with missionaries in personal ways. They are often hungry for pastoral care and are eager to drink in whatever I may have to share. Very often I find them spent and dry. They live their lives at such a high level of output that there are few opportunities for them to find refreshment.

Quite often, the conversations include a confession

that they simply do not think they have anything left to give. They are considering leaving the field, frustrated with circumstances or feeling spent. Invariably I make this difficult request: "Tell me about your prayer life." Almost always they will respond by saying, "I pray." Then I ask, "When do you pray?" "Well, I pray all day. I pray before meetings, I pray before meals, I pray before bedtime. I pray with my kids. I pray when things come up. I pray before a challenge or a roadblock."

I then press in and ask when they schedule time to pray just to develop intimacy with the Father. When is their hour each day in close communion with Him? What time of day have they sanctified as their non-negotiable abiding time with the Lord? Many do not have such a practice. It is not that they think it is unimportant; they all know it is. They simply allow the details and emergencies of life to crowd out the most important thing they can possibly do each day and every day.

Jesus said that apart from Him we can do nothing: "I am the vine; you are the branches. If you remain in me and I in you, you will bear much fruit; apart from me you can do nothing" (John 15:5). He also said, "If you remain in me and my words remain in you, ask whatever you wish and it will be done for you" (John 15:7).

Our enemy, the devil, knows the most powerful thing we can do is to abide in Christ. It is in these intimate, daily prayer times and our close communion with Him that we feel His heart for the lost. We gain His passion for the mission and we find the power to do all that He calls us to do. It is not the education, the training, or the brilliant mind that will accomplish His will; it is His Holy Spirit who can do all things working through us.

If the devil can get us to rely on our expertise and abilities and distract us from devotion to prayer, then he has successfully neutralized us as effective warriors in the greatest contest in the universe. The battle to pray is frequently just that: *It is a battle to pray*. We think of the battle as some titanic struggle in prayer against lofty spiritual powers, causing us to pray long and hard for specific items.

To the contrary, Jesus said that the Father knows what we need *before* we ask (see Matthew 6:8). The battle is sometimes a struggle in heavenly places but it is frequently the struggle to get out of bed to pray. It is a fight every day to get to our hour of prayer or better yet, two hours of prayer. The enemy will try to derail us with emergency emails, sick babies, traffic, and many other legitimate distractions. We must fight through all these to get to the primary work of God's people—prayer.

Jesus prayed. That seems like an obvious statement and a little silly to state, but think about that for a moment. He was God, praying to God. He was the Creator of the universe and yet He relied on the Father for His directions. If Jesus found it necessary to pray and receive His insight and power to do God's will through prayer, then certainly we need His power and insight far more than Jesus did. Prayer is not an option for the people of God; it is a necessity. It is more so a necessity for ministers and missionaries.

This is such an important issue that I will devote the entirety of the next chapter to continue our discussion of the importance of a vibrant prayer life in the preparation of your candidates.

## chapter five

# LAP TIME

You might guess that this topic of prayer is front and center in the development of my missions candidates. I was discussing with Elliott, one of my candidates, this kind of relationship I wanted him to pursue with the Father. He was explaining to me how difficult it was for him to do this because after 10 or 15 minutes, he ran out of things to say and to pray about. I explained to him that this is the point. We need to pray until we have nothing left to pray about.

When we stop jabbering at the King of the universe and reach the point where we no longer have advice for Him on how He should do things, then we have finally reached the point where we can abide in Him. God does not need advice on how best to manage the universe, friends, family, or our jobs. He already knows.

Many of our prayers are really commands to God to do something. This seems highly inappropriate to me. I would never enter a courtroom and demand that the judge put my neighbor in jail because she offended me. I would not march into the office of the CEO of the company where I work to instruct him or her on how he or she should deal with a competing company or with my officemate. In our arrogance, we actually think the Lord needs our advice. He does not.

Yes, we are commanded to make our requests known to God. This is entirely appropriate. We are also commanded to pray without ceasing and to intercede on behalf of the church, its leadership, and the lost. In Philippians 4:6, we are told that "in everything by prayer and supplication with thanksgiving let your requests be made known to God." As important as these prayers are, this is not what is meant by the word *abiding*.

## WHAT IS ABIDING?

In an attempt to explain to Elliott what the relationship looks like that God wants with him, I used the illustration of my granddaughters. I have 13 grandchildren and I love them all, but my relationship with my granddaughters is different than with any of my grandsons. On the all too rare occasions when I get to spend extended time with my grandchildren, it will frequently occur that one of my granddaughters, Philomena, Lyla, Evangeline, Rowan, or Isabella, will crawl up onto my lap and snuggle in close to my chest and just sit there allowing me to hug and hold her. Sometimes I hold her for three minutes before she jumps off and runs away; sometimes she will sit there for an hour or until she falls asleep.

During these times, we may have simple

conversations. I may ask some silly questions and get simple answers. She may tell me about her pink shoe-laces that Mommy bought her, or how she went to the playground and saw a friend. It really does not matter what we talk about. The value of the moment is the relationship. Never yet have any of my granddaughters informed me of some great matter. We have not discussed philosophy, science, theology, or any other complex topic.

The exchange happens on a very deep and unspoken level. Words do not matter. Conversation is unnecessary and irrelevant to the moment. And yet, these are some of the most treasured moments of my life. These are certainly the most treasured of any of my interactions with my granddaughters. I love this time with them and they love it with me. They feel my strength and tenderness. I am blessed because they love me. I would spend a hundred hours doing this if possible.

This is the relationship we need to develop with our Father. This is where I push my candidates to go. This is where the deep longing for Christ is born and develops. This is what I refer to as abiding. This is where the Father downloads His wisdom, insights, revelations, love, and passion into our hearts. This is where we hunger for more of Him. It is not in our instructions to Him, it is in the context of our passionate longing for more of Him. This is where our best prayers happen without a word being spoken.

Frequently when I am praying for our missionaries, I do not have words or information that will allow me to pray with any knowledge. I do not know their current circumstances and the most recent communication I have may be two months old. Nevertheless, I can still pray relevant prayers without needing words. Often, I simply intercede by stating their name and holding them up to the Lord while my soul groans within me on their behalf. He knows. He loves them more than I do. He does not need my advice. I simply lay them on His altar and ask Him to hear them, and I hold them up to Him until He releases me to move on to the next one.

Elliott decided to name what I am describing as his "lap time." This depth of relationship with God does not happen by accident. It happens because we are intentional and because we intensely pursue it. Hebrews 11:6 informs us that God is a rewarder of those who diligently seek Him. The most rewarding thing I do every day is sit on my Lord's lap. My schedule has 7:00 to 8:30 every morning blocked out for my lap time with God. I cannot wait to get to my office to meet with my Father. I awake every morning longing for His presence.

This is where God empowers my ministry and inspires me. This is where He fills me yet again with His Holy Spirit. This is life to me. When I miss this time, I feel dead and sluggish. When I miss this time, my ministry is heavy and difficult. When I miss this time, I find that I am working and striving in the flesh, and my work is a burden.

## Teach Them to Pray

This chapter is an appeal and apologetic for the most important thing you will need to do for your missions candidates, and anyone else whom you mentor: Teach them to pray. Force them into a disciplined life of prayer. Have them read the prayer books of E. M. Bounds, Bill Hybels, or others.

If you were to ask any of my missions candidates I am mentoring, "What is Glenn's first question to you at every meeting?", they would all respond by saying that I ask them about their prayer life. I expect them all to develop a habit of spending at least an hour every day in prayer. This is the source of their life and power in ministry. Without this, they are weak and anemic and incapable of doing in the Spirit what the Lord calls them to do.

Jesus said, "Very truly I tell you, the Son can do nothing by himself; he can do only what he sees his Father doing, because whatever the Father does the Son also does. For the Father loves the Son and shows him all he does" (John 5:19-20). He also said, "For I did not speak on my own, but the Father who sent me commanded me to say all that I have spoken" (John 12:49).

How is that possible? We know it is true because Jesus said it, but how is it possible that He was so tuned to the heart, mind, and thoughts of the Father that He could say He *never* did anything except what the Father did? It was made possible through His prayer time with the Father. Jesus was certainly distracted with the daily duties of living, just as we are. He had to eat and socialize, buy clothes and shop for food, and do all the other mundane things that everyone else had to do.

Yet His relationship with the Father was so close and intimate He could say that all His words and actions were the Father's. Luke 5:16 tells us, "But Jesus often withdrew to lonely places and prayed." This was His habit, as we also learn from Matthew 14:23, Mark 1:35, Luke 6:12, and Luke 9:28.

If we are to be like Jesus (and we are), we must be so closely attuned to the Father that we approach being able to say these same words. Jesus heard the Father while in His times of prayer. He prayed all night on the mountain. At other times, He moved away from the crowds so He could pray, going off to solitary places. If Jesus, the God and Creator of the universe needed to pray, how much more is our need to pray? Prayer is a reminder that apart from Him we can do nothing.

The Apostle Paul commanded us in Romans 12:12 to be constant in prayer and again in 1 Thessalonians 5:17, he urged us to pray without ceasing. If these are commands in Scripture, then we can be certain that this was a hallmark of the life of Jesus, the perfect man. I do not think the meaning of these verses can be better articulated than it has been done by John Piper in his *Desiring God* series in which he stated:

> The word "constant" here doesn't mean that every minute you are praying. It means persist in prayer. Persevere in it. Stay at it. Be devoted to it. Don't give up or slack off. Be habitual. It's the opposite of random, occasional, sporadic, intermittent. In other words, Paul is calling all Christians to make prayer a regular, habitual, recurring, disciplined part of your life. Treat prayer the way you treat eating and sleeping and doing your job. Don't be hit and miss about it. Don't assume it will fill in the cracks of other things. Dealing with God in prayer deserves more than a dial-up on the fly.

## An Illustration

Several years ago, I was working with a seasoned missionary who had been on the field for many years. This missionary was working in a field that was spiritually dark and closed to the Gospel. Besides that, he was working to rescue kids from sex trafficking and was confronting government and criminal resistance to his efforts to release young people from this wicked bondage.

I had been training a young candidate who was a counselor and wanted to join him on the field to minister to these deeply damaged children. All arrangements had been made and dates were set to deploy this counselor to the field when things seemed to stall. There had been so much resistance to this ministry for so long from so many areas that the level of frustration and fatigue among the team was such that they were inclined to give up.

After several months of little communication with the missionary and no clear direction of how to proceed with this eager candidate, I was finally able to connect. I asked what was happening and why communication had seemed to abruptly terminate at such a critical moment. The missionary, dejected and apologetic, stated that instead of bringing on a new missionary partner and counselor in three months, they were planning to close up shop in three months. This was January and he stated that he expected to close the doors by April.

We talked at some length and I expressed my sadness and sympathy. At some point during our transoceanic call, I felt impressed to enquire, "Hey, tell me about your prayer life." He said the very typical "I pray. I pray a lot. We always pray before meetings," and on and on.

I said, "No, tell me about *your* prayer life." He said that sadly he had lost his prayer life. He did not pray as he should, only offering a quick prayer in the morning and another one before lying down at night. He was faithful in Bible study and devotions with the team, but they did not pray much together.

I told him that I wanted him to promise he would commit to pray first thing every day for one hour. During that time, he was to pray to express and enhance his intimacy with the Father but also for the rescue mission. I also told him I wanted a promise that he would lead his team in daily intercession for these entrapped youth as well as the ministry. Also, he promised they would all engage in warfare against the enemy that wanted these children enslaved and tortured. He was remorseful and the Lord opened his eyes to see that this had been a serious neglect on his part. He promised to do all that I requested, but then did even more.

Two days later, I received a request from him that our missions committee at the church would fly his team to a weeklong prayer conference in another country. Our church's missions committee readily agreed and paid all the expenses. He then requested another weekend retreat to do the same and the mission committee again obliged. (What a great missions committee we have at ACAC, led by deeply committed and devoted people. If you don't have a missions committee, I suggest that you build one. They will become one of your church's best missions assets.) He was good to his promises and led his team into passionate intercession and devoted personal and corporate prayer. Consequently, his team was transformed. Where previously there was discord, unity grew.

In April, three months after our phone conversation during which he had predicted that they would be closing the doors to the ministry, he called again and expressed good news through tears of joy. In the intervening three-month period, all the hindrances and blockages plaguing this ministry for years had dried up. The Lord fixed every government licensure issue, every tangle of red tape, every threat, and every resistance in every sector, all because they prayed earnestly and with expectation.

The point is that despite all the gathered expertise represented by the team in that country, despite their credentials and determination, they needed to pray their ministry success into existence, remembering the truth that "the weapons of our warfare are not carnal, but mighty through God to the pulling down of strongholds" (2 Corinthians 10:14).

The best thing you can teach your candidates is to make prayer an essential part of their lives. Make them dependent on prayer. Create a hunger in them for the presence of God. Lead them on until they pant after God as the deer pants for the brooks of water. Keep after them. Help them know that their life and power are to be found only in Him as they abide in Him.

## INTERCESSION

Aside from personal intimacy with the Father, teach your candidates to intercede. Many of us do not know how to do this well. We can get a glimpse of the meaning of intercession by reading James 5:13-20. In that passage, James directed our attention to Elijah who was a man just like us and yet who prayed earnestly that it would not rain—and it didn't rain. This is intended as an example of how we ought to intercede.

When you send your candidates to the field, they must know that the effectual fervent prayer of the righteous person avails much. They must know that intense cries to the Lord on behalf of those who are perishing will be heard on high.

After a business failure in 1986, I found myself in debt and broke. It was a steel-related business in which I had invested heavily. While awaiting the outcome of the longest and last strike of the United Steelworkers in the Pittsburgh area and immediately prior to its loss of the entire steel industry, I took a job driving trucks for a local company. I had hoped it would be a temporary job, but months stretched into years.

While working at the job, I met another believer who was also a driver. We both talked about how difficult it was to begin a conversation about God in the climate of the rough-and-tumble, blue-collar world of teamsters. There were other believers who were more effective at sharing their faith but both of us were having difficulty. He suggested we pray for our coworkers and customers.

I cannot take credit for the idea; it was his suggestion that started this ball rolling. Thereafter, we began to meet every other Tuesday evening for two hours just to pray. We began to make a list of the people we sensed the Lord was placing on our hearts. We continued to pray twice a month for two hours each meeting.

After several weeks, something strange began to happen. People with whom we had not been able to find an opening to talk about faith or religion soon began to corner us and ask questions like, "Hey, are you a Christian? Will you pray for my wife, she needs surgery?" or "You are a Christian, right? I have a question." This happened again and again. We added more people to the list and every week we had growing opportunities to share the love of Christ.

To the best of my recollection, we were able to

pray with, witness to, or respond to a faith question with every person who was on that list. It was one of the most remarkable things I had ever seen. It taught me a powerful lesson that God does the work of convicting and drawing people to Him through us. We only speak the words. We cannot compel anyone to enter the Kingdom. The best that we can do is to intercede.

This will also be a valuable lesson for your candidates to learn. Their ministry will depend on their devotion to intercession. At my church, we were seeking to start a ministry to an unreached refugee population that had settled nearby. They have a different language, culture, and religion. We had no idea how to begin reaching out to these needy people, and so another minister and I began to pray.

We prayed for two years for the Lord to guide us and to open doors of opportunity. We prayed for one hour every morning, five days a week for two years before we began to see any progress. We have finally seen an explosion of ministry among those people over the last three years. Thousands of hours of service have been devoted to these neighbors by hundreds of people from our church as well as several other local churches. The foundation for the work was and is prayer.

Teach your candidates to access the power available to them through intercession. Teach them to be dependent on the Lord for their ministry, for guidance and direction, for individuals, for events, projects, and organizations. The more they intercede before they deploy to the field, the more they will see God's faithful answers to their prayers.

## Fasting

The discipline of fasting has a diminishing appeal

in 21ˢᵗ century America. Our self-indulgent and over-stimulated appetites rebel at the thought of deprivation. We do not want to delay any gratification and we hate the thought that we may need to be uncomfortable or unsatisfied in the short term to achieve a higher cause or goal in the long term.

I will not make a defense of the biblical discipline of fasting. If you have ever read your Bible, you have noticed that there are more than 70 references to fasting. I also will not try to construct a comprehensive argument to convince you that fasting is a necessary discipline, even though it certainly is. Instead, I will point you toward the many excellent books and papers written on the matter.

In Mathew 9:15, Jesus declared that once the bridegroom was taken away, His disciples would fast. Paul and Barnabas were sent out on their first missionary trip because of God's direction during a time of prayer and fasting in Acts 13:

> While they were worshiping the Lord and fasting, the Holy Spirit said, "Set apart for me Barnabas and Saul for the work to which I have called them." So after they had fasted and prayed, they placed their hands on them and sent them off (Acts 13:2-3).

There are numerous benefits of and purposes for fasting in the Bible that include: seeking God's guidance, adding "horsepower" to our prayers, humbling ourselves, repentance, deliverance from temptation, protection, deliverance from enemies, worship, grief, dedication to God, developing intimacy with the Father, success, and victory.

Fasting is a regular part of normal Christianity.

It was a normal practice in the early church and it has been a normal and accepted aspect of worship and intercessory devotion throughout church history. Anglicans fasted on Fridays. Charles Wesley refused to ordain any pastor who refused to fast on Wednesdays and Fridays. In his *Institutes*, Calvin stated, "According to the need of the times, [pastors] should exhort the people either to fasting or to solemn supplications, or to other acts of humility, repentance, and faith" (Book four, chapter 12 of Calvin's *Institutes of Christian Religion*).

Fasting is necessary because of the massive impact it has on us individually as well as the power it brings to our supplications. We all must fast. Jesus fasted for 40 days before the beginning of His ministry. If He needed to fast, so must we.

Because of Satan's unrelenting resistance and the assaults your candidate will face while on the field, it is necessary that they learn how to make fasting a regular part of their lives and ministry. You need to teach them to fast as a regular part of their disciplines as well as for specific needs and initiatives.

I have seen the power of fasting in my own life and ministry many times. Several years ago, an 89-year-old woman called my home and asked me if I would officiate her funeral. She stated that she had inoperable brain cancer and it had spread to the point where the doctors gave her no hope of recovery. She had tumors throughout her head, down her neck, and across her shoulders. She was too old to risk chemotherapy or radiation, so her doctors advised her to go home and love her grandchildren and they would keep her as comfortable as possible during the three remaining months they gave her to live.

I responded that I would be honored to do her funeral if she died, but requested that I come and visit her as soon as possible. I went to her home and expressed that the Lord is Lord of everything and that I was going to pray He would heal her. I shared the Gospel with her and promised to come to her home every Tuesday evening to pray with her and her husband.

During this first meeting, the Lord moved me to fast on her behalf and therefore I began to fast the following day. I expected this would be a short fast of a few days, but the Lord did not release me from the fast for 28 days, a full four weeks. I did not eat any food at all for 28 days. During this time, I interceded for her and her family.

After several weeks, she seemed to be in brighter spirits. When she went to visit her doctor, he took some x-rays and found that her tumors were shrinking. The doctor was amazed and stated that he had no explanation for this phenomenon. She responded that she and her pastor were praying for a healing. This trend continued for the next six months.

At every doctor visit, the tumors were a little smaller. Eventually after six months, the doctor told her that he could still see some dark spots where some of the tumors had been but that they were all gone. She died several years later of an unrelated illness, but cancer-free. I attribute this in part to my willingness to obey my Lord when He called me to intercede for her with prayer and fasting.

Several of us at our church fast on a semi-regular basis. We do it for personal edification as well as for ministry success and the advancement of the gospel. Several years ago, three of us sensed God calling us to a month-long fast in December. We were encountering a great deal of resistance in reaching out to a refugee community in our city. We all sensed that we were facing spiritual resistance and so we went to war through fasting and prayer.

Throughout the month of December, we fasted and resisted all the goodies and delicacies of the holiday season. We understood that we were doing warfare for the souls of many people enslaved by a false demonic religion. My two comrades-in-arms received great spiritual encouragement while on this fast. They spoke daily of new insights and revelations in the Word as well as in personal intimacy with the Father.

On the other hand, I had none of that. My month was heavy and laborious. I did not receive any insights, nor did I sense that I was drawing closer to God. I was just slugging through a difficult and dry time. Halfway through the month, the Lord gave me a vision of myself, in which I was scraping and plowing hardpan earth behind a mule with a single spade plow. It was hot and hard work and the plow was barely scraping the surface of the hardpan. For the remainder of our fast, I had this vision every time I prayed. It never seemed to improve; it was just hard work.

At the end of our fast we all debriefed, and I listened as the others told of deep and tremendous insights because of their dedicated time with God. I remember telling my fellows that I felt farther away from the Lord than I had at the beginning of the fast. Within a few short months, however, we began to see progress among the refugee community for whom we had been fasting. Doors began to open and within the year we saw an explosion of ministry and services to this community. As I was praying one day, the Lord revealed that this fruitfulness in ministry was the result of all the plowing that had been done the previous December.

I tell these stories because they are representative of many similar stories that can be told by those who have made fasting a part of their life and ministry. Fasting reminds us that it is the power and presence of the Holy Spirit that does all the ministry. Fasting reinforces our awareness of our dependence on Him. We tend to default to our own capacities, but fasting affirms our awareness of His sufficiency our reliance on Him. For that reason, it is an essential though neglected spiritual practice for those who are called to the missions front.

## Pray and Fast for Your Candidates

Though candidates may present you with what seems like confusing and bewildering puzzles, sorting out their calling is a life-defining matter that God wants them to understand. It is more than a career choice or a decision about what major to choose in college. The decision will require significant life changes in every imaginable way. Approach this matter of clarifying the call with the utmost gravity, but also with confidence in God's ability to make it clear because *He wants them (and you) to know.* Use the lack of clarity as a means of teaching your candidate a deep reliance on Christ as they seek Him for direction, which He must provide.

As I write, I have walked with God for more than 40 years. I share with all my candidates, along with anyone else who will listen, one important thing I have learned from God in those years. Every time I have been confronted with a dilemma, a choice that is not clear, a fork in the road, or any opportunity for which

I am seeking direction or clarity, I always go to God in prayer seeking His answer.

I pray and sometimes fast, asking God for clarity and His answer in all circumstances has always been the same. He says, "Come closer to me." So I pray more and fast more and His response is, "Come closer still." He is always drawing me closer to Himself and He uses the uncertainties and dilemmas in my life to get my attention and draw me into a deeper, more profound, intense, and intimate communion with Himself. As I press into Him with more passion and intensity, as my hunger for Him swells within me, and as I make Him my goal and my sufficiency, He then reveals the answer I have been seeking.

You see, God is not worried about the details of our lives, for He already has them worked out and planned. He is more interested in us becoming as passionately in love with Him as He is with us. He wants us to love Him with our whole heart, soul, mind, and strength. This is His ultimate goal for you and your candidate.

Therefore, walk through this task of clarifying the call with your candidates and pray with them. Seek God and fast with them. You have an opportunity to teach your candidates a valuable lesson that will sustain them through all the challenges their lives on the field will throw at them. Teach them how to find the heart and mind of God through intimacy with Him.

Remind your candidates that the Lord wants them to know His will for them. He is eager to show them when, where, and what. They will find His will in the throne room sitting quietly in His loving embrace.

## Train the Candidate to Expect Miracles

If I have one stunning observation from my travels

to the field, it is that so many missionaries have such little expectation for miracles. Even missionaries living among primitive people accustomed to seeing demonic displays and signs too often do not have confidence that the God of the universe is greater and eager to display His power through them.

I know of missionaries who are living in dark places and who have been the victims of demonic attacks. They know the attacks are demonic and orchestrated by the enemy, but they do not know how to counteract them. They remain the victims of a lesser power because they have not learned how to fight in the spiritual realms through the unlimited power of the ultimate Power who inhabits them. Romans 8:11 makes it clear that the Spirit who raised Jesus from the dead inhabits our mortal bodies. First John 4:4 states, "Greater is He who is in you than He who is in the world."

Too many missionaries go overseas expecting that they will be able to do God's work without His power. Their seminary training may have convinced them that it is incorrect or unrealistic to expect to see God's power displayed. Their theology may even dismiss the fact that God is still in the miracle business.

I assert that it is not only possible to expect the miraculous, it is absolutely necessary, and it is your job to introduce your candidate to the supernatural elements of ministry. You must teach them to conduct deliverance ministry, to pray for the sick and the infirm, and to pray for the impossible.

When you conduct deliverance at your church, call your missions candidate to sit in and have them participate. Teach them that they never need to fear any demon anywhere. There is no power any demon has that can overcome the power of God in them. Teach them how to differentiate between the demon-possessed and the afflicted. Help them understand the power of prayer and fasting in deliverance.

Take them with you when you go on home or hospital visitations. Allow them to pray in faith for the sick and to comfort those who are facing death. Allow them to experience the miraculous here so that it becomes a natural part of their understanding of ministry. When they see the sick healed here because they prayed and asked for a healing, they will be encouraged to rely on the miraculous overseas.

There is no place on earth where demons are not actively resisting the Gospel. They work to frustrate and discourage ministers and missionaries. They attack the families of the saved and unsaved. Do not allow your candidate to go into international, global warfare without knowing who the enemy is and how to fight him.

The fact is that our enemy is already defeated. He has no power over the saved except that which we yield to him. His power was broken at the cross. He is defeated and the world is waiting for the revelation of the sons of God who will take this earth back from the grip of the enemy and will proclaim freedom to the captives.

As already mentioned, it is important that our candidates pray and intercede and also learn to fast as important spiritual disciplines that will help them fight His battles in His power. This should be with a worldview that God still performs miracles of healing and deliverance as well as miracles of changed hearts and converted souls. God hears our prayers and our candidates should not only pray but expect answers and changes as a result of their prayers—both in their own lives and the lives of others.

There are other spiritual disciplines that are important if our candidates are going to be successful in the field, so let's turn our attention to them in the next chapter.

## chapter six

## MORE SPIRITUAL DISCIPLINES

When runners are preparing for a marathon, they are in training that involves more than just running. They must pay attention, not only to their training to run, but to every aspect of their health: diet, sleep, clothing, shoes, and water intake. The same is true for your candidates. In addition to prayer and fasting, there are many other spiritual disciplines and habits they must develop if they are going to run the race well on the mission field. In this chapter, we will look at three more: rest, Bible study, and personal growth as expressed in the concept of self-awareness.

### A SABBATH

In a sense, the issue of rest is related to the issue of prayer. Often the biggest hindrance to both a prayer life and a regular Sabbath rest is making or having the time to pray or rest. You must help your candidate understand the importance of a Sabbath for them. They must learn to recognize their need for restoration as they pour themselves into ministry and people with desperate needs. Teach them to make this practice a permanent part of their lives.

As ministers of the Gospel, we and our missions candidates will find that our Sunday responsibilities are anything but restorative. We are engaged in the Lord's work all week and especially on Sundays. Therefore, participation in Lord's Day activities and worship hardly qualifies as a rest from our labors. What do we do to find a refreshing break from our labor?

This is a question worthy of an answer, for it has serious repercussions for our ministry effectiveness. I know of missionaries who are doctors in remote missions hospitals. They are overworked and understaffed and every call on their time is an urgent life-and-death demand. What's more, the demands are non-stop, any hour of the day or night.

Besides being urgently needed at the hospitals, they are also urgently needed at the local churches. They are the only people around who have formal educations as well as access to Bible-study helps, commentaries, and biblical knowledge. When they go to church, they are often expected to be the teachers.

Who is pouring into their lives? When do they get a break? Unfortunately, the answer too frequently is no one and never. These people are prime candidates for burnout and ministry fatigue. Everything they do with too little sleep and too few resources drains them even more. This may seem like an extreme situation, but it is common among many missionaries.

You must help your candidate find the practices, diversions, activities, sports, or recreational pleasures that allow for life to be restored to them. It may be solitude or a rousing concert, a run in the jungle or a trip to the city. Whatever it is, teach them to admit, own, and protect it.

## BIBLE STUDY

As with all the topics covered in this book, Bible study may already be a well-established habit with your candidate. If so, simply hold him or her accountable and keep yourself well-informed of what they are studying and reading so you can discuss areas of interest, conflict, disagreement, or revelation. Discussions with the candidate regarding their Bible studies will allow you to understand where they may depart from orthodoxy and a sound, accurate comprehension (and application) of the texts.

It may be, however, that the person you are mentoring is unfamiliar with the entire Bible. This has occurred in my experience on several occasions. One of my mentees was raised in the church and came from a good Christian home where biblical principles were part of daily life. She had been active in student ministries and had been exposed to sound teaching and sermons. She had read much of the Bible and had read through the New Testament several times, but had not yet ever read through the entire Bible.

As a result, she had not yet confronted the wrath of God in the Old Testament. She had not yet encountered the harsh judgment of Moses' sin or the brutal conquest of the Promised Land. My requirement for her was that she join me in a year-long reading of the entire Bible. We used the *Mission 119* Bible-reading program and commentary produced by Reverend John Soper.

I also asked her to keep a journal of questions, insights, concerns, and conflicts that she encountered while reading and studying. This gave me a great opportunity to discuss the nature of our God as well as the often confusing realities of His interactions with humans.

In the current moment of missiological strategic thought, there is a growing reliance on marketplace types of ministry. There are opportunities for professionals and business people to go to places where traditional missionaries are unwelcome. Though many of these passionate and devoted people are well-seasoned, well-educated, and astonishingly successful in their chosen fields like engineering, counseling, or marketing, they often have a poor or insufficient grasp of Scripture, doctrine, and theology. They are capable of acquiring all the necessary capacities without going to seminary, but they may need you to help guide them.

Perhaps your denomination has a training institute. It may not be accredited like a college or seminary, but is sufficiently thorough to prepare candidates for a sound education they can apply to their work in the field. My denomination, the Christian and Missionary Alliance, has such a training program called the Ministerial Study Program (MSP). The MSP is designed to develop character, biblical knowledge, and competency in basic but important ministry skills.

It is also a good idea to require your mentee to lead and teach a Bible study. There are few things as fundamental to ministry as the capacity to plan for and conduct a fruitful, ongoing Bible study. This is a skill that will serve them well here at home as well as on the field. Teach them how to do a basic inductive Bible study. If they have never been a part of an inductive Bible study group, then take them through one so they can understand what it is and how to prepare ahead of time for the study.

There are many online research tools available today. Make certain your mentee has a familiarity with these tools. Help them become familiar with the various commentaries that are available as well as the denominational, doctrinal, and philosophical perspectives of the authors. Hold your mentee accountable. Ask direct questions about their time in the word of God. Stress with them the importance of their personal devotions. Help them to develop a passion for the word of God.

I like to do an extended study of Psalm 119 with them. This is the psalm that stresses the love of the Word, statutes, Law, and precepts of God. It declares again and again that the laws of the Lord are the source of life, that we are to rejoice in following His statutes, and that we long for His precepts and delight in His laws. A study, understanding, and love of this psalm will pay dividends in the life of your mentee and will lay a foundation that will sustain them through their future trials and passions.

Make certain that you are modeling for them this passion for the Word. If you are not daily in the word of God and meditating on the Scripture, do so. It is insufficient for you to substitute your sermon prep for your personal passion for the Word. Preparing for a teaching is important but is not the same as allowing God to speak to you through His Word. You must be a lover of the Word to be able to transfer this love to another.

Hold yourself accountable or consider asking someone else to hold you accountable. You cannot lead another where you have never gone. When you fall in love with the word of God, it will be a contagious condition that everyone around you will catch, especially your mentee.

## Self-Awareness

I include the concept of self-awareness in this chapter because it is a vitally important spiritual practice. That may seem strange to you, but let me explain. If the candidates don't have an accurate assessment of where they are spiritually (or where they are not), they can self-destruct on the field or at least encounter serious problems.

The Apostle Peter had to develop this awareness because of his near-fatal failure during Jesus' betrayal and death. In Mark 14:31, we read that Peter said emphatically, "'Even if I have to die with you, I will never disown you.' And all the others said the same." Peter was not alone in his overestimation of his spiritual condition. Of course, we know that he denied he even knew Jesus a few hours later.

Furthermore, we also know King David did not cultivate self-awareness of what was in his heart that motivated him, for the sordid tale of David and Bathsheba is a story of legendary failure. After that incident, David wrote, "Behold, You desire truth in the innermost being, and in the hidden part You will make me know wisdom" (Psalm 51:6 NASB). Your role as a mentor is to position the candidate to search for the truth of who they are and the reality of their heart at any given time—before they go and while they are in the field.

Let me share a personal example. If there is such a thing as a workaholic, it is I. I want to work all the time. I am accustomed to 12 to 16 hours of work every day and if I work less, I feel uneasy and useless. The licensing and ordination requirements for the C&MA include a three-year period of time after licensing and prior to ordination during which every candidate must be mentored and supervised by ordained persons in the district where they minister. I was blessed to be mentored in the Western Pennsylvania District of the C&MA by Reverend Jim Krause and supervised by Reverend Jeffery Norris, the district superintendent at the time.

During the pre-ordination period, we had many duties to complete. One of the duties was to keep a journal of activities for an entire week twice a year for the three years. My journal recorded my typical twelve-plus hours of work per day, five days a week, plus week-end duties of typically 10 or more hours. If I added it up, my average workweek had between 60 to 80 hours per week.

After the second journal of the second year, Pastor Norris sat down with me and pointedly asked, "Why do you work so much?" I was confused by the question. I had always worked long hours. My response was, "Well, there is a lot to do."

He followed my answer with a more curious question, "Why?" Again, I didn't understand the question, so I responded, "Because there is a lot to do."

He asked again, "Why?" This went on for some time while my slow brain struggled to comprehend what he might be getting at. After all, good people work and work hard. If there is nothing to do, they invent things to do. Idle hands are the devil's playground, and so on.

After a painfully long time of struggling with the point Jeff was trying to make, he told me the story of Bob. There was a man who had a fish tank in his office, which was the home for a fish he had named Bob. Every morning, the man entered his office and greeted Bob with the same question: "How is the water today, Bob?" Every day Bob would respond with the question, "What water?"

The point Jeff was trying to get my dull mind to realize is that there is something behind the compulsions that drive me that I may be completely unaware of, simply because it is normal for me. Like Bob, it is the environment in which I lived and was raised that determined how I thought about myself and how I structured my life so that I could be comfortable with who I believed Glenn to be.

I'll give a brief history of Glenn for illustration. My father, his father, and his grandfather all died suddenly at 39. My father died when I was ten years old. It was a sudden and unexpected heart attack that took his life. I had two older sisters and one younger sister. While sitting at the funeral home next to my sisters and looking at my dead father lying in the casket, and having been sternly warned to sit still and keep quiet so that I did not upset my grieving mother, a long procession of people walked past us children.

Virtually every person who addressed us did the same thing. They would pat my sisters on the head or kiss them and express regrets and sorrow at their loss. When they came to me, the only boy, they would straighten up, shake my hand or pat me on the head and say things like, "Well. you are the man of the family now. You have some big shoes to fill. Your dad was a good man, and now your mother will be relying on you to be the man of the house." They also informed me that "big boys don't cry."

Since every person, without exception, said the same things to me without exception, as a ten-year-old I was certain that all these statements were true. Even though I was unsure of how I would do my father's work and fulfill his responsibilities, it was clear that it was up to me to do so. Immediately, lots of things did fall on me, like all the male chores around the house like cutting the grass.

By the time I turned 12, my grandfather pulled me aside and said, "I am beginning to think that you are no damn good." Befuddled, I asked why. He said, "You are already 12 years old and you do not even have a job yet. You need to start bringing money into this house to take care of your sisters."

The next day, I got my first job. I worked throughout my high school and college careers. By the time I turned 14, I was able to get working papers that allowed me to work 20 hours per week. I soon learned how to manipulate the system so that I could use the papers in more than one place. I was working 40 hours per week using those papers at two local fast food stores and pumping gas in my spare time at a local garage for additional hours. Every penny I earned, except for the little I kept for myself to buy cigarettes or go on occasional date, I brought home and gave to my mother for the running of the household.

During those days, my mother frequently vented her frustrations and anxiety about her responsibilities as a single mother on me. I repeatedly heard that I would never be half the man my father had been and I would never amount to anything. I would also never be half the man that my grandfathers or uncles were. I was lazy and useless to her. If I slept in on the morning after going to school the previous day and then working till 10:00 that evening, I was accused of being lazy. Apparently, a 16-hour day at 15 years of age qualified me for the title "lazy."

My response to all this was that I vowed to be twice the man that my father, grandfather, and anyone's uncle had ever been. (I am sorry to say that I failed in that personal goal as well as many others). Part of that strategy was to outwork everybody else. Furthermore, I vowed that if I ever had a family, I would have them well taken care of by the time I died at 39.

It became my goal to be so wealthy that I would retire at 38, coast through 39, and hopefully live to 40. (Oops, a couple of more missed goals.) Hence, I became a workaholic. My abnormal work ethic was normal for me and I could not see it. By the way, God had other plans for me. I had two businesses fail and I had the worst year of my life at 37, was flat broke at 38, and still lived through to 66 at the time of this writing.

This is my story, but you have one as well—and so do those you are mentoring. There are things in your past and in your family life that have shaped and caused you to act and react in ways that may not be righteous—or are dangerous to your health or spiritual well-being. Your ethics, morals, preferences, defenses, and dozens of other things have been shaped by your normal. They have developed in the water of your environment just like Bob the fish.

The same is true for your missions candidates. There are things that your candidates do that seem normal and good to them, but may be corrosive and destructive and will fail and melt them when they get to the furnace of overseas missions. Dr. Rob Reimer states in the introduction to his *Soul Care* seminars that we can never rise above our own level of self-awareness. On the webpage for his organization Renewal Ministries International at http://renewalinternational.org/soul-care, he has made this statement:

> Brokenness grasps for the soul of humanity. We are broken body, soul, and spirit, and we need the healing touch of Jesus. *Soul Care* explores seven principles that are profound healing tools of God: securing your identity, repentance, breaking family sin patterns, forgiving others, healing wounds, overcoming fears, and deliverance.

I highly recommend Dr. Reimer's book, *Soul Care*, and suggest that you take your missions candidates through it. It will be even better if you take them through the book *and* the DVD series in the context of a small group. Organize a group of people to work together through these resources. It will provide a cleansing context and help reinforce an awareness that these issues are common to all people and that good Christians need to be set free from some strongholds.

There are lots of good resources for this work. Another Reimer book is entitled *River Dwellers*. It addresses the problem that we all face of maintaining a deep and consistent connection with the Father. The premise of the book is that we can live in the river flow of the Spirit of God but that we too frequently and for many reasons get out of the river. Rob helps us understand when we are out of the river, why we are out of it, and how to get back in. Your candidate needs to know how to stay wet in the river of God's presence.

There is another aspect of self-awareness that is important as the candidate prepares for deployment. That is the concept of their personal strengths and weaknesses as expressed in their individual personality. Let's look at that concept in the next chapter, along with the suggestion that you not mentor alone, but enlist the services of an effective counselor to help in this pursuit of a candidate's self-awareness.

## chapter seven

# LIFE SKILLS

The concept of personality is approached from different angles in the Christian world. Some discount personality as having much importance because they believe the Spirit can empower people to do anything they are called to do. I disagree, not that the Spirit will empower, but that candidates can become anything they set their mind to be. God gave them a personality and that will greatly impact their work.

Some who come to you love details and administration, while others do not. Some are naturally more skilled working with people. Still others love to multitask and are able to work quickly, while some are more deliberate. Some enjoy making big decisions and others avoid them. All this will have an impact on the work they do, and the more you can help them understand their personality, the more effective they will be when they enter the field.

## PERSONALITY AND STRENGTHS

Most of us enter our fields of service by accident rather than through intentionality. Your missions candidates may come to you with a deep conviction that the Lord has called them to the mission field but they have no idea what they are to do or where they are to go. If you ask them what they want to do, the answer may be something like, "I don't care, I just want to serve the Lord."

It is your job to assist them in finding what the calling looks like. This does not need to be a random search or a matter of leafing through a missions book that lists available options. It also does not need to be limited to fields where the candidate already has some training, experience, or education.

I know a woman who needed to reenter the workforce after having been away for many years raising children as a stay-at-home mom. She went to a job fair at a local community college to consider her options. At the job fair, she took a *StrengthsFinder* assessment profile. The results indicated that she would fit well into accounting or computer programming, two fields that had never occurred to her as possibilities. On the basis of this tool, she pursued an education in computer programming and has risen to the top of her field. She was not only well-equipped for the position, but she loves it and has found great joy in her success.

Assessment tools can be a wonderful resource to help your candidates find a context for their calling. Three of the tools that I employ are the DISC, Gallup *StrengthsFinder,* and the SDI Assessment Tool. I do not know if these are the best tools available or the only ones that should be used, but they help me open discussions that help the candidates understand what their strengths and limitations might be.

For example, if a person tests as being an S or C on the DISC profile, it may be a poor fit to suggest to them that they apply for a director position in a new field to start a brand-new work. Their personality, which tends to be more cautious with the desire to follow established set patterns and rules, will probably not allow them to be successful. They are outstanding followers but not always risk-taking leaders.

## GET ACQUAINTED WITH A GOOD CHRISTIAN COUNSELOR

I cannot overemphasize the importance of this point, for you will not be able to assess or equip your candidates by yourself. Having good Christian counselors available who are willing to sit and talk with me about the various candidates helps me do my job well. Sometimes something will come up in a meeting with a candidate that will cause me concern. It may be the candidate's response to pressure at work or a comment made in passing.

I do not always recognize when a red flag has been raised and I sometimes see a red flag when there isn't one. It is always helpful to consult with people who are smarter and better educated than I. If I think I do see a red flag in the candidate, I am eager to make a referral to a counselor whom I trust to evaluate quickly and accurately. I would rather err on the side of caution than send someone overseas uncertain of their stability or health.

For example, I had a young candidate who had

been raised in a family where the father had a long-term illness. The stress that the illness brought on the members of the family elevated the tensions and responsibilities for everyone. The intense nature of the illness brought about many urgent and threatening emergencies.

This produced in the candidate a calm and placid demeanor that seemed unusual. When a personal emergency arose in her life that severely threatened her health, she had a benign and indifferent response to it. I was alarmed and asked her what she thought about the matter. She responded by saying, "Oh well, if I go blind, I go blind. It is God's will and I will live with it."

I was having none of that response for it seemed to be strange. I called on a counselor whom I know well and asked her to see the candidate for ten sessions, which she did. As I do with all my candidates, I required her to sign a release allowing the counselor to discuss freely discuss with me anything that was discussed in counseling.

After seven of the ten sessions, the counselor called me up to make an appointment to discuss the candidate. Her evaluation was that the candidate was as right as rain. She concluded that the candidate did not need any more sessions and that she was satisfied after only seven. This was just her normal. Having grown up in her family of origin with all the chaos and ongoing emergencies, she had developed low-energy, non-panicked responses to events that others would consider extreme.

This situation illustrates why it is important to get the input of others. I have available to me a pool of outstanding counselors who know what I am looking for. I have met with them and discussed my goals for and role with my candidates. I do not send candidates to counselors for therapy, although that sometimes will happen in the sessions. I send them for evaluations.

I have educated the counselors on the extreme pressures common on the mission field and have informed them that we need to send only healthy people to the field. We do not send perfect people, but we do want to send healthy people. All issues do not need to be resolved, for some take a lifetime to do so. The candidates need to be in a position, however, where the issues will not destroy them and they have the tools for appropriate resolution.

Where do you find such valuable people to help you? We have a local service called the Christian Counselors Collaborative. It is a clearinghouse of Christian counselors who are trained and licensed, but who minister from a biblical and Christian perspective. I am close friends with the leader of the Collaborative who has made recommendations of counselors eager to help in this important work. He recognizes the value of this work to the extent that he has found funds to provide scholarships to cover the fees for the candidates I recommend. This is valuable because most candidates are lacking the funds necessary to pay for these vital services.

There is probably a similar counselor or group of counselors near you who will be eager to provide a similar service. Search them out and be clear about what you are looking for. Educate them on the pressures related to missions work so they have a context for what you are asking them to do. If there is nobody in your hometown who can do this work for you, perhaps your denomination can recommend someone. It is possible to do these evaluations long-distance through Skype or video calls. We have been able to arrange for long distance and even cross-cultural counseling between people on different continents.

If you are not able to find scholarship funds for your candidate so they can get these necessary evaluations for free, approach your church and ask for funds. This is a beautiful way for the church to invest in missions in a practical and valuable way.

If after the evaluation by the counselor you consider that the candidate is not yet healthy enough to proceed to the field, *do not give up* on the candidate. Remember that this is one point in time on the long continuum of their lives. All you have really learned from the counselor is that there is more work to be done. The work may involve counseling, deliverance, forgiveness, repentance, or dozens of other things, but hang in there with your mentee and assume that God is able to do a miracle.

## chapter eight

# MINISTRY SKILLS

You have a great opportunity to download into your candidate the years of ministry experience and skills you have acquired. You know how to lead people to faith in Christ. You know how to ask questions that bring a person to a moment of truth. You know how to turn a conversation to a faith challenge. Teach these things to your candidates.

Many missions candidates have dreams of winning for Christ some foreign nation without access to the Gospel. They dream about opening their mouths and hundreds will come running to hear what they have to say. They dream of great throngs hungering for the good news, so they go off to the field with high hopes and little experience.

Many have never even led another person to faith

in Christ. Some may not have witnessed to their co-workers. Others will not have shared their faith with their families. It is your job as their mentor to ground them in reality of where they are and what to expect when they go.

Take them with you when you go places and allow them to see how you share your faith with strangers and in casual encounters. If you have a team at your church that conducts evangelism, hook the candidate up with these people. A great way to train your candidates to share their faith is to encourage them to volunteer with CRU, formerly Campus Crusade for Christ. These young people are passionate about sharing the Gospel anywhere. They have strategies and techniques that enable them to strike up meaningful conversations with strangers. When you send your candidates overseas, make certain that they are passionate about and skilled in winning the lost.

Nik Ripken, the author of the amazing book, *The Insanity of God*, has stated that "90% of those born in the church, raised in the church, saved in the church, married and buried in the church will never share Jesus with another person." This is an appalling statistic. It is probably true and if not, it seems to be true. There is an ethic in America that it is impolite to talk about religion in public. Furthermore, it is considered insensitive and off-putting to others and therefore we ought not to discuss religion out loud. This is not a Christian ethic. Instead, we are to shout the good news from the rooftops. We are to carry this Gospel to the ends of the earth.

It is possible that your candidate has been poisoned by American religious ethics. You need to find out if this is so and if your candidates are not sharing their faith, that must change. You need to force the issue and push them past their comfort zone. This idea of religious politeness is a toxin that will not only kill the initiative of your candidate on the field but also may spread to the entire team, rendering them impotent and useless as missionaries. The truth is that if your candidates are not sharing their faith here in the States, there is little likelihood they will share their faith overseas.

I once visited a field that was fairly closed to the Gospel. It was not dangerous to share the Gospel; there was simply an intellectual and cultural bias against Christianity. I was visiting with several missionaries at a party-like reception and sat down next to a seasoned missionary. I asked him how he was doing and how the ministry was going. He looked me in the eye and stated matter-of-factly, "Well, you need to be in this country for eight years before you can share the Gospel with anybody."

He then looked a little puzzled and turned to his spouse to ask, "No, we have been here for nine years, haven't we?" He corrected himself by saying, "You have to be in this country for nine years before you can share the Gospel with anybody." I wanted to throw up. I realized that this couple had been living overseas on other people's money and generosity but they were not doing what they were being paid to do.

I do not know the circumstances of their lives on the field or what may have caused them to become ineffective. It may have been fear, failure, or lack of motivation or training, but they were wasting Kingdom money while taking advantage of other Christians. This would have been unacceptable in the business world.

No company would pay anybody to live overseas at great expense for nine years and accept no production whatsoever.

The remarkable thing is that I was in the country for less than a day when I had an opportunity to share the Gospel with a room full of people who had asked me why I was there. Force your candidate to be a soul-winner or disqualify them from service overseas unless they are going to serve as an accountant or another type of support staff.

## Make Your Candidate into a Leader

As a mentor, you are acting in the place of a parent in many ways. One thing a parent must do is force their children into duties and practices they must master in order to be successful adults. Teach your candidates to be leaders. Help them understand that without leadership, nothing gets done.

If they have a fear of people, help them get past it. If they have a fear of public speaking, coach them through it so they can share the Gospel in season and out. If candidates are shy and retiring, teach them to be bold and decisive. Go out of your way to put them in positions where they must take leadership in the church and other situations. Entrust decision making to them and then walk them through the outcomes and consequences. There are many good leadership books available that will be helpful to read and discuss with your candidates.

Teach your candidates to disciple others. Train them to be able to pour their lives into the people in your church. Select others in the church who are hungry for leadership and counseling, and place them in the care of the candidates. In all likelihood, mentoring and discipleship will become an important part of their ministry overseas. It will be helpful for them to learn how to mentor under your tutelage.

Find areas of ministry where you can entrust your candidate with team leadership. Perhaps you would like your church to develop an outreach initiative. Help your candidates to conceive an idea and then nurture them through the planning phase. Allow them to recruit volunteers, raise funds, plan, and execute. Afterwards, debrief and help them improve as they imagine their next project.

## COUNSELING

A big part of any ministry is counseling. This is not something that comes naturally to many people. When possible, invite your candidate into counseling sessions with others. Allow them to observe and take notes. Discuss the sessions with them afterwards and allow them to understand your thoughts and strategies. Teach them how to listen and to actively ask questions, how to hear what is *not* being said, and to uncover underlying issues. Encourage them to take classes that will enhance their skills in counseling.

## CROSS-CULTURAL UNDERSTANDING

Your candidates will probably receive some cross-cultural education and experience through their sending agency. If that's the case or not, you can jump-start or supplement the process by seeking out internationals in your local community and then help your candidate befriend them.

Encourage them to take responsibility for being an advocate for local immigrants and refugees. Help them think through what a refugee-service ministry might look like. Maybe a food or clothing ministry would be helpful. Perhaps they need to learn English as a second language. Being an English-speaking partner for a recent immigrant is a wonderful way to build friendships and will open the door to many opportunities to share their faith.

Encourage your missions candidates to make friends at the local university that will certainly have international students eager to make American friends. Encourage them to host internationals in their home and share holidays with them. I frequently hear people say that there are no internationals in their hometown. That is probably not true but if it is, there certainly will be in a nearby town. Send your candidate out to find them.

## SHORT-TERM MISSIONS

If the candidate has never been on a short-term missions trip, now is the time. If the candidates have an idea of where in the world they are being called, send them there. Send them through a reputable agency with which you are familiar. Better yet, organize one for them. Include people from your church who may be interested in supporting the candidates in their future deployment.

Be certain to provide a good pre-field training for the trip and the candidate. I like *CultureLink*, which is well-written and comprehensive. We have used *CultureLink* training for all our short-term trips at ACAC for the past ten years. Prior to implementing this training, we had several short-term trips that did not go well. They were poorly planned and led, and we had little guidance or few policies to govern any short–term trips. Since implementing the curriculum, we have not had any bad trips at all. There are other good training curriculums as well, so just do your homework and find one.

After arranging for the candidate to go on a short-term trip, the next step is to teach him or her to lead a short-term trip. This will allow the person to learn valuable leadership skills in a cross-cultural setting. *CultureLink* also has a training seminar for short-term trip leaders. This will be a great opportunity for your mentee to learn and immediately put into practice the things that he or she learns. If your candidate has not sat through any cross-culture courses in college, it would be helpful for you to assist him or her in finding and taking a course at a local Christian college or online.

We are almost finished with my approach to mentoring a missions candidate, but there are still a few more loose ends I would like to wrap up in the next chapter before I share some final thoughts, along with an Addendum outline of all that we have covered. Let's wrap up those remaining loose ends, what I call nuts and bolts, in the next chapter.

I named this chapter "Nuts and Bolts" because there are some additional practical things you can do to help your candidate that are important for you to know about.

## PERSPECTIVES ON THE WORLD CHRISTIAN MOVEMENT

If you have not taken the 15-week *Perspectives* course, you should consider doing so and then encourage your candidate to do so as well. More people have taken this college course than any other in history. It is a course designed around four vantage points or perspectives. The missions perspectives are from biblical, historical, cultural, and strategic vantage points.

Though I do not consider this to be a requirement for each candidate, it is helpful for all. The course enables the candidate to see that they are a part of a 6,000-year-old, God-driven, global strategy to fill the Earth with the glory of the Lord. This effort crosses denominational lines, political boundaries, governmental philosophies, and every other man-made distinction.

This course is not only valuable for every candidate but also for every missions mobilizer. Some churches require that every elder and ministry leader take this course. We will soon be offering *Perspectives* at our church on an ongoing basis and will encourage the entire congregation to consider taking it.

## A Road Map for Deployment

Your candidate is as unfamiliar with how to proceed to become a missionary as you may be. They have heard and responded to a call from God and then have approached you because they consider you to be the expert (ready or not). This is a great trust they have already placed in you. There are several elements with which you will need to assist your candidate.

## Understanding the Call

I have had only one candidate over the past 10 years who has come to me with a clear and certain call that included a time frame, a place, a people group, and a task. Most come to me stating they know that the Lord has called them to serve overseas but they do not know where, when, with whom, or what they should do.

Some candidates have come with a little more clarity. I have had some state that they feel called to use their counseling, nursing, business, occupational therapy, anesthesiology, or some other training overseas but they do not know where. Others have come stating that they feel called to India, South America, Spain, Thailand, or elsewhere, but are not sure what they would do there.

Still others have come with clear certainty that the Lord has called them to work with orphans, children sold into sex slavery, or the poor, or they know the Lord has gifted them as an evangelist or church planter—but they do not know where or when. It is now your job to help them discern and flesh out the nature of the call on their lives. How will you accomplish this very important task? There is no easy answer, but there are some things that you can do.

## INTRODUCE YOUR CANDIDATE TO MISSIONS LEADERS IN YOUR WORLD

This is an important practice. My denomination, the Christian & Missionary Alliance, is one of the finest missions-sending organizations on the planet. I am biased I know, but it is also the opinion of others. You may disagree and prefer your own denomination and I support your claim—while holding on to mine. In the C&MA, we have more than 700 full-time missions servants in the field. The C&MA started in the U.S.A. but has grown through missionary focus over the past century, so that the C&MA is larger around the world than it is in the United States.

This means that I have available to me and my candidate hundreds of people who eat, sleep, and work in missions all the time. We have missions-candidate development specialists who are eager to meet and help to develop my candidates. We have global strategists who are eager to meet with new candidates to discuss opportunities that I cannot even yet imagine.

We have missionaries from all around the world who are willing to mentor my candidates if I can make the arrangements. The C&MA has three colleges, all of which have missions faculty members who are interested in helping to guide and equip my candidates. Your denomination probably has resources that you will want to access on behalf of your candidate. Do it. If not, call the C&MA in Colorado Springs.

## FIND AFFINITIES AND STRENGTHS

In Chapter Seven, we discussed the value of personality and gift profiles. This is also applicable here. Use the results of the profiles to discuss and help your candidates imagine or consider things that may not otherwise have occurred to them. For example, if they have always loved working with children, this may be a good indicator of an area in which they can serve. If their skills are administrative, there is a huge need for these gifts on the field almost anywhere in the world. Help them think outside of their experiences but in keeping with their gifting.

## RESEARCH MISSIONS JOB POSTINGS

Our denomination has far more missions openings than we have candidates to fill them. On the webpage for the C&MA, many job descriptions and opportunities are posted. Not all available job listings are even posted because there are more than can be listed. This is also true of most other sending organizations. Encourage your candidate to research missions opportunities around the globe.

## CONSIDER INTERMEDIATE SERVICE

There is an old saying that God cannot steer a parked car and it may be applicable in the matter of helping your candidates discern their call. In our denomination, there is an organization called Envision with both domestic and international sites that sponsor short-term ministry opportunities. They also have intermediate opportunities for candidates to serve as interns from six months to two years. It may be a good option for your candidate to do a year or two of intermediate service to help them determine their long-term calling. In an overseas placement, they may discover where their strengths and passions lie.

Adventures in Missions (AIM) has an interesting program called the World Race. I have had several candidates sign up for this challenging, year-long world tour. They visit 11 countries around the globe in twelve months. The participants have an opportunity to serve in various types of ministries in each of the countries they visit. Two of the three candidates we have sent on the World Race have benefited greatly by learning of their strengths and passions, and two of them are now serving overseas as full-time missionaries.

## SEARCH OUT MISSIONARIES ON HOME ASSIGNMENT

Be an advocate for your candidate. Keep your eyes open for missionaries who are on home assignment to whom you can introduce your candidate. Let them rub shoulders with missionaries and ask questions. Be intentional about setting dates and meetings. Most missionaries are eager to encourage other similarly-minded people. Allow your candidate to ask questions about their calling and how the missionaries discerned their own call. This will help take some of the mystery out of the process.

It is also helpful for the candidate to learn that missionaries are not super people with supernatural hero powers. They are simple, ordinary people doing extraordinary things through the power of the Holy Spirit. Encounters with other active or retired missionaries will help to demystify the process of discerning the call.

## MARRIAGE AND FAMILY

Your candidate may be married, soon to be married, or married with children. In any case, it will be necessary to meet with and develop your candidates as a family. Everybody must be on board. It a serious matter if one family member is reluctant or opposed, and this must be resolved. If both spouses are not convinced of their call, I will not send or approve them for overseas missions work. The challenges are far too great for the individuals and their marriage to thrive or even perhaps to survive. Both spouses must be certain of the calling to missions.

The relationship between husband and wife is clearly stated in Scripture as a depiction of Christ's relationship with the Church (see Ephesians 5:22-32, Galatians 3:28, and 1 Corinthians 12:13). As such, the appropriately well-ordered, loving, and healthy Christian marriage of a missionary couple is a witness to the culture where they are going. In cultures where women are considered second-class or chattel, a Christian marriage is an illustration of Christ's sacrificial outpouring of love on behalf of His beloved. In post-Christian societies where marriage is an anomaly, a loving, committed, and faithful Christian marriage is a beacon of light shining in the chaos and loneliness of confusion, betrayal, and brokenness.

A missionary marriage must be healthy and strong. As a candidate mentor, this is also part of your business because only a healthy marriage can withstand the pressures to be encountered on the field. It is your business because a fractured or unhappy home will undermine the words and work of the missionaries. The people will see the dissonance of a sermon of peace and reconciliation spoken out of a marriage of turmoil and disrespect. Marriages must be strong and godly.

The picture of a wife appropriately and happily submitted to the authority of her appointed head and husband is a beautiful illustration of the happy submission of the believer to his head, the Lord. Likewise, the loving, generous, and self-sacrificial kindness and affection of a husband toward his wife paints an appealing and inviting picture of the kindness and love of our God.

Furthermore, the home is a haven, especially on the field. The family will face many challenges and pressures while deployed. The home must be the refuge and safe place for all family members. When there is chaos without, there must be peace and faith within. This will start while the family is still here in the States prior to deployment. Hold your candidates accountable for having family devotions. Teach them to have family conversations and times for honest communications. Observe them in many and varied circumstances so that you can coach them well.

It will be helpful to send them to Christian marriage seminars or marriage encounters. At our church, there are several *How We Love* classes offered every year, as well as classes on the five love languages. Make use of these resources or sponsor your own.

If you see things in the marriage that seem beyond the scope of these types of classes, it does not necessarily disqualify the candidates. Make use of the counselors that you have befriended and get them some marriage counseling. I repeat that they must be healthy *before* they deploy. There will be plenty of opportunities in the future after deployment for you to speak into their marriage if you effectively establish your relationship with them at the beginning. When they encounter marriage problems, and we all do, you will be the person they turn to in confidence if you do this well at the beginning.

## Choosing a Sending Agency

Not every sending agency is well run, responsible, or even reliable. You do not want to send your candidate through an agency that is ill-prepared to care for the needs of your candidate. I have had some of our candidates sign on with agencies that mishandled their funds, failed to pay their salaries, and misrepresented the nature or success of the work on the field—-along with other outrages. I even had one agency intentionally misrepresent itself as Christian while abandoning the doctrine of exclusivity. Be very careful.

You may not be able to find good information about an agency. After all, there is not a *Consumer Reports* type of screening organization that handles sending agencies, but do all you can to investigate. Even some of the large and reputable agencies are ill-equipped to intervene in a crisis. Many agencies are poor at member care, and may not be concerned for the welfare of your candidate once they deploy to the field. This may land on your plate to handle ongoing care while your candidate is deployed.

It may be that your options are limited. In some areas of the world that are hard to get into, there may only be one or two agencies that are active. If possible, meet with the president of the organizations and ask lots of questions. Go into any relationship with your eyes wide open and fully understand the agency's weaknesses and shortcomings. Do not assume they do all things well. I always prefer the C&MA and try to direct my candidates to work with them if possible. I believe they are the best in the business but they are not in all places or doing all things.

## LANGUAGE

It is necessary that missionaries be fluent in the local language. As soon as the candidates have decided the part of the world to which they will deploy, get them started in language training. Most agencies require several years of language training before a candidate can fully engage in the work on the field. The sooner this training starts, the better.

## DEBT

The C&MA will not send a missionary to the field who has excessive debt. Most young people graduate with a large college debt that will take years to pay down. If they deploy to the field with this debt, then a good portion of their resources must be used for their debt, which will leave them little available for living and ministry expenses on the field.

Therefore, it's important that you help your candidates eliminate debt. This can be done in a number of ways. Help them find low-cost or free housing. Perhaps a family in the church would be willing to provide a room in their home. Help them find low-cost transportation; perhaps the church would be willing to help them pay for an inexpensive vehicle. It may be appropriate for the church to hire the candidate to do some ministry work. If the church has embraced this candidate with your recommendation, perhaps the church will allow the candidate to do some fundraising or will contribute funds to help pay down some of the debt. Whatever you do will be greatly appreciated and a great encouragement. Be an advocate for your candidate.

## EDUCATION

It may be that after your candidate has articulated a call to missions, there will be a need for additional education. It could be that a high school senior has approached you to inform you of the call. Help him or her think through what an appropriate education may look like. It could be cross-cultural, pre-med, fine arts, or almost anything else. You will want to have an appropriate level of input with the student and the parents. You will also want to stay in touch with the candidate through their college years.

Perhaps the candidate requires additional post-graduate education to deploy to the field. Help the candidate think through the available options. Your input will be valuable and greatly appreciated. You may be able to help them access scholarships or other assistance that is available to the candidates through your denomination or other interested parties. Use this as an opportunity to build a deeper and lasting relationship with your candidates.

## PERHAPS YOUR CANDIDATE IS NOT CALLED TO THE FIELD

This is a real possibility. It does not mean that they are not useful in ministry elsewhere. Through the course of your interactions and relationship with the candidate, it may become clear to both of you that missions is not the right answer. Perhaps the candidate got fired up and excited at a rally or missions conference and thought there was a call on his or her life, but it becomes clear they were mistaken. This is actually a victory. It is far better to learn this here in the States prior to the expenditure of lots of Kingdom capital and misspent years of their lives than to go overseas and discover it through a tragic failure. If this is the conclusion, then you have served God and the candidate well.

## You Can Do This

This is not an impossible task. If I can do this, anyone can. Allow the Lord to guide you through this important work. Develop your reliance on Him in these matters.

Pray diligently for your missions candidates. There are a hundred things I have not addressed in this book. It would be impossible to name every possible issue that must be addressed. This book is simply a strategy for thinking about how to mentor a candidate well.

The goal is to get the candidate healthy enough to grow and prosper in their calling. If you can help them do this, you will have served them, the Kingdom cause, the lost overseas, and the Lord well through important pastoral service. In my mind, there is no more important work, and let me share with you why I think that is true in my final chapter that follows.

## The Heart of the Matter:
## Fostering the Souls of Mission Candidates

When I considered a title for this book, the choice of the word *fostering* was quite intentional. Fostering carries the idea of raising a child who is not your own through birth. It means to love, encourage, nurture, promote, cultivate, strengthen, enrich, empower, and commit to, along with many other nuanced expressions of advancement and service.

Look at this exquisite passage which gives us a tender and revealing glimpse into the heart of the Apostle Paul. His service was neither a career choice nor a duty, but rather a loving, fulfilling, and joyful sacrifice on behalf of others:

But we were gentle among you, just as a

nursing *mother* cherishes her own children. So, affectionately longing for you, we were well pleased to impart to you not only the gospel of God, but also our own lives, because you had become dear to us. For you remember, brethren, our labor and toil; for laboring night and day, that we might not be a burden to any of you, we preached to you the gospel of God. You are witnesses, and God also, how devoutly and justly and blamelessly we behaved ourselves among you who believe; as you know how we exhorted, and comforted, and charged every one of you, as a *father* does his own *children*, that you would walk worthy of God who calls you into His own kingdom and glory (1 Thessalonians 2:7-12 NKJV, emphasis added).

This beautiful depiction of the ministry of the great apostle also describes the characteristics of our own modern ministry. It is tender and kind. It is gentle like a nursing mother, affectionately longing for the well-being of the object of her affection. The warm-heartedness and self-sacrificial nature of the mentor involved in candidate preparation is not to be compromised. This relationship is the incubator for the global warrior.

The context of Paul's relationship with every one of the Thessalonians was also one of direction and exhortation. As a loving father, Paul personally engaged every one of them in encouragement, comfort, direction, and instruction regarding their behavior.

As mission mobilizers, the task to which we are called is eternally significant. We educate our congregations about the greatest call to battle in the history of the universe. We must seize every opportunity to model and advocate on behalf of our God's mission, properly called the Great Commission. If we do not affirm and elevate the call to missions, the call will go unheeded and unfulfilled.

The work that we do has not only eternal consequences for individual souls, it has eternal consequences for the advancement of God's kingdom here on earth. Jesus taught us to pray, "Thy Kingdom come, Thy will be done on Earth as it is in heaven" (see Matthew 6:10). The will of the Father is to see all men saved and to come to a knowledge of the truth (see 1 Timothy 2:4).

We, the Church, are the equivalent of the Old Testament children of Israel. They were brought up out of oppression and slavery and then appointed to conquer the Promised Land and to restore the reign of God on earth; now we are commissioned with proclaiming God's kingdom through Christ. Their objective was the promised land of Canaan; ours is the entire world. They were redeemed by the blood sacrifice of countless animals; we were purchased by the blood of Christ and set free from the oppression of the enemy so that we can go forth to conquer on our Lord's behalf in the power of His Holy Spirit.

To continue the comparison, Joshua was promised that the children of Israel would possess all the land on which their feet trod (see Joshua 1:3). We also are guaranteed victory, for in announcing the Great Commission, Jesus promised to be with us to the ends of the earth (see Matthew 28:19-20). We also are sent out to wage and win God's warfare against all the powers of darkness. We are told in Ephesians 6:12 that we wrestle "against principalities, against powers, against the rulers of the darkness of this world, against spiritual wickedness in high places." These are some of the greatest and most powerful beings the Lord ever created. Not only are we to wrestle, but we are also to relish the contest and run to the battle. We are to eagerly engage the enemies of our God and rejoice and triumph in the victories.

Jesus promised Peter that the gates of hell would not prevail against the Church. The Church wins this victory by the power of God, and individual Christians always win against Satan and his empty-headed demons, provided the Christians know they are in the battle and are willing to fight. Satanic power is broken, and the power of the God of the universe resides in each one of us.

The only way the Church can be defeated is if it stops warring and does not engage the battle. That is what much of the 21st century church in the U.S. has done. It has become consumed by the lie of fulfillment through wealth and prosperity on this earth. God promises fulfillment, not in this life, but the next. Some maintain that the church is a resort where people can find peace, safety, entertainment, wealth, and happiness. Jesus said that He came not to bring peace but a sword to counteract and combat the culture and spirit of the world.

Jesus referred to us as an assault force that will knock down the defensive gates of hell to plunder the enemy camp of captive souls. To our shame, the Church in the U.S. has lost its message, its will to fight, and its certainty that the lost are truly lost. We have stopped teaching sacrifice and instead teach prosperity. The result is that millions are dying while believing the lies of the enemies of our God and we do not care enough to do what our Lord has called us to do.

You, oh mission mobilizer, if you do your job well, will facilitate the salvation of millions of people who will stand before the throne in eternity. When you determine to equip the workers for the harvest (which Jesus promised is ripe), you are a dangerous enemy to the adversaries of our God. The power you wield in equipping and sending healthy missions candidates to the field will reap fruit throughout this age and into the next.

Because of the mandate of Christ, you *must* do this. With the help of Christ, you *can* do this. If I can do this, anyone can. Allow the Lord to guide you through this important work and develop your reliance on Him in these matters.

As I urged you earlier, pray diligently for your missions candidates. There are many things I have not addressed in this book, for it would be impossible to name every possible issue that you must address. This book is simply a strategy and guide for thinking about how to mentor a candidate well.

Your goal is to produce candidates healthy enough to grow and prosper in their calling and to rejoice as they plunder the enemy. When you equip them to do this, you will have served them, the Kingdom cause, the lost overseas, and the Lord well.

## GUIDE FOR FOSTERING MISSIONS CANDIDATES

The following pages contain a summary checklist
of the topics discussed in this book for
quick and easy review.

**I.** Get to know the candidate

    A. Establish a regular meeting time to:

        1. Discuss to clarify and understand the nature of the candidate's calling

        2. Learn about their life history and background, and become familiar with their current life

        3. Understand habits, education, personality, strengths, weaknesses, and fears

    B. Personal development

        1. Build trust

    2. Explore family of origin background, siblings, and parents

    3. Learn about formative events, disease, disappointments, passions, sexual background, abuse, neglect, encouragement, and sources of strength

  C. Relationship with God

    1. Worship patterns

    2. Prayer and Bible study habits

    3. Sabbath and rejuvenation.

    4. Where do they get refreshment? Restorative time?

**II.** Self-awareness

  A. Strengths and weaknesses

    1. DISC profile

    2. Gallup *StrengthsFinder*

    3. SDI Assessment tool

  B. *Deeper Life Training* by Rob Reimer

  C. Find and work with a competent Christian counselor

**III.** Intimacy with the Father

  A. Bible study

    1. Scripture

      a. Memorization

      b. *91 Weeks* program or other study with commentary

      c. Bible-reading plan

      d. Inductive Bible study

      e. Availability and use of commentaries

   2. Prayer

      a. Disciplined prayer time

      b. Listening prayer

      c. *The Power of Prayer* by E. M. Bounds

   3. Sabbath

      a. What does it look like?

      b. Discipline

   4. Intercession

      a. For ministry

      b. Guidance

      c. For individuals

      d. For events, projects, organizations, etc.

   5. Fasting

   6. Miracles

**IV.** Ministry skills

   A. Doing evangelism

   B. Leading a Bible study

   C. How to disciple

   D. How to lead a team

**V.** Cross-cultural understanding

   A. Cultural adaptability

      1. Get to know internationals

      2. Host international students

      3. Befriend international students and immigrants

   B. Go on short-term missions trip

   C. Lead short-term missions trip

   D. Take course in cross-cultural training, i.e. *Culture-Link*

**VI.** *Perspectives* class

**VII.** Theological orthodoxy

    A. Studies in Christian doctrine, Trinity, Virgin Birth, salvation, justification, etc.

    B. Holy Spirit

        1. Power

        2. Word gifts

        3. Personal giftings

    C. Christology

**VIII.** Determine course for ministry preparation

    A. Education

    B. Choosing a sending agency

    C. Ordination

    D. Area of the world

    E. Language

    F. Introduce to the C&MA

**IX.** Spiritual warfare instruction, training, and books

    A. Any book by Neil T. Anderson

    B. *The Power of Prayer*, E. M. Bounds

    C. *Too Busy not to Pray*, Bill Hybels

    D. *Outline Studies in Christian Doctrine*, George F. Pardington

    E. *River Dwellers*, Rob Reimer

    F. *Soul Care*, Rob Reimer

    G. *Power of Mentoring*, Martin Sanders

    H. *Bondage Breaker*, Neil T. Anderson

    I. *Parents of Missionaries: How to Thrive and Stay Connected When Your Children and Grandchildren Serve*

*Cross-Culturally,* Cheryl Savageau and Diane Stortz

J. *Insanity of God,* Nik Ripken

Special Note: A great read on candidate development with another excellent book list of reading suggestions is *Skills, Knowledge, Character: A Church-Based Approach to Missionary Candidate Preparation.* Greg Carter, Turtle River Press, 2010.

Glenn Hanna has served as missions pastor at Allegheny Center Alliance Church in Pittsburgh, PA since 2008. Glenn responded to a call to ministry at the age of 55 after spending his career in business. Therefore, his approach to ministry has been influenced by his years in construction and heavy industry. Glenn has been married to his wife Patty for 25 years and they have five children and 13 grandchildren.